# Menace

...plumbers kn...

"Sure, ... forward. "Do you have a deck o...

"Silence, fool!" shri... the giant turtle. Quickly he reaches into his robe and pulls out a handful of old, dry bones. He flings them in front of the plumbers.

"Fork, knife, come to life!" he chants.

The bones begin to swirl around, as if trapped in a miniature tornado. Then they suddenly organize themselves into two huge turtle skeletons.

"Dry Bones. Oh, no!" moans Mario.

The horrible bone monsters stomp toward Mario and Luigi.

"Smash them!" orders the magician.

**What will happen to the plumbers now?**
**It's up to you to make the decisions that will get them through this fiendishly fun adventure!**

# Nintendo® Adventure Books
## Available in Mammoth:

**DOUBLE TROUBLE**

**LEAPING LIZARDS**

**MONSTER MIX-UP**

**KOOPA CAPERS**

**PIPE DOWN!**

**DOORS TO DOOM**

**DINOSAUR DILEMMA**

**FLOWN THE KOOPA**

# Nintendo® ADVENTURE BOOKS

### FEATURING THE SUPER MARIO BROS.®

## FLOWN THE KOOPA

By Matt Wayne

Dear Gimp,

enjoy trying to solve Dinosaur Dilemmas and watch out for Kirby in the Monster mix-up!

**MAMMOTH**

Happy easter
Love boyle.

*This book is dedicated to Dr. Carole Karp*

First published in the USA 1991 by Pocket Books, a division of Simon & Schuster
First published in Great Britain 1992 by Mammoth an imprint of Reed Consumer Books Ltd
Michelin House, 81 Fulham Road, London SW3 6RB and Auckland, Melbourne, Singapore and Toronto

Reprinted 1993

ISBN 0 7497 1309 7

A CIP catalogue record for this title is available from the British Library

Printed in Great Britain by Cox & Wyman Ltd, Reading, Berkshire

Creative Media Applications, Inc.
Series developed by Dan Oehlsen, Lary Rosenblatt & Barbara Stewart
Art direction by Fabia Wargin Design
Cover painting by Greg Wray
Puzzle art by Josie Koehne
Edited by Eloise Flood
Special thanks to Ruth Ashby, Lisa Clancy, Paolo Pepe & George Sinfield

# Dear Game Player:

You are about to guide me through a great adventure. As you read this book, you will help me decide where to go and what to do. Whether I succeed or fail is up to you.

At the end of every chapter, you will make choices that determine what happens next. Special puzzles will help you decide what I should do—if you can solve them. The chapters in this book are in a special order. Sometimes you must go backward in order to go forward, if you know what I mean.

Along the way, you'll find many different items to help me with my quest. When you read that I have found something, such as the tickets, you'll see a box like the one below:

> ### ***Mario now has the tickets.***
> ### Turn to page 50.

Use page 121 to keep track of the things you collect and to keep score.

Good luck!
Driplessly yours,

*Mario*

# 1

"The cookies are done!" sings Toad, the royal mushroom retainer. He gallops along the deck of the royal cruise ship carrying a tremendous tray of fresh-baked chocolate chip treats. "The cookies are done! Get your red hot—AHHHH!"

Slipping on the S.S. Moreltania's red shag carpeting, he stumbles forward and falls head-first down a small flight of steps. Cookies scatter in every direction as Toad lands with a thud.

Princess Toadstool and the Super Mario Bros. rush to help poor Toad. But then Luigi is distracted by the sight of his friend Yoshi making a dash for the cookies.

"Hey! No fair!" shouts Luigi, as Yoshi scoops up two dozen cookies with a lap of his tongue.

The six-foot-tall baby dinosaur sticks out a slender green arm and snatches five more cookies.

"Those were mine!" whines the tall, skinny plumber. He stomps around the cabin angrily, picking up any crumbs he can find.

1

"Relax, little brother," says Mario. "I'm sure Toad will bake some more." He picks Toad's polka-dot hat up off the cabin floor and places it gently upon the stunned mushroom retainer's head. "As soon as he recovers from his fall, that is."

"What happened?" asks Toad, gazing blankly at Mario and Princess Toadstool.

"You just had a little mishap," the princess informs him. "Don't you remember?" She pauses to straighten her emerald medallion. "You fell when you were running with the cookies."

"Cookies?" Toad says curiously. He gazes around the lavishly decorated ship's cabin. He looks up and studies the large chandelier hanging from the center of the ceiling. Then he stares directly into the princess's blue-gray eyes.

"Who are you?" he asks dully.

"Oh no!" howls Mario. "He's blown out his memory!" The super plumber takes off his cap and runs one hand through his bushy hair.

Luigi looks around the cabin nervously. "Who's going to bake more cookies?" he asks.

Meanwhile, two flights above, on the S.S. Moreltania's control deck, the Mushroom King is hard at work steering the ship toward Dinosaur Island, where the International Dino-

Flying Derby is about to begin. Seven hours ago, the ship left its dock in the Mushroom Kingdom. The king pressed the "Automatic Pilot" button and hasn't taken his eyes off of the big, red switch ever since.

"Boy," he remarks, shoving back his gold and purple crown. "This is even tougher than ruling the Mushroom Kingdom."

Everything seems to be running smoothly. The chief mushroom assistant, Wooster, is back home at the castle, making sure everything stays neat and clean. The Super Mario Bros. are with the royal party, in case anything goes wrong. Everyone already has tickets for the Derby, so there shouldn't be any trouble getting in to see the show. The princess is even passing out spending money to everyone, so they can buy popcorn at the Derby. And if the Derby is anything like all the posters say it will be, the royal party is going to have a wild time.

"Yes, sirree," the king says to himself. "For once, everything is under control."

***The plumbers have the pair of tickets and 10 coins.***
Turn to page 93.

# 2

Luigi stays where he is. No matter how hard the magician tries, he can't reach him.

"Arrgh," growls Magikoopa. Luigi can hear his voice echoing high overhead. "There's more than one way to sink a plumber."

Suddenly, there is a flash of blue light. Magikoopa appears on the floor in front of the startled plumber. He's shrunk himself too!

"Now I've got you!" the turtle screams.

Luigi darts from underneath the TV and begins to climb up the side of the set. By the time he reaches the top, though, Magikoopa is right behind him and gaining fast.

"Geronimo!" shouts Luigi. He dives into the opening on top of the TV.

**If the plumbers have the remote control, turn to page 61.**

**If they do not have the remote control, turn to page 69.**

# 3

"R-r-a-rr," Luigi growls, as he and his brother march out of the boat wearing Mega Mole costumes. "I'm a big, scary monster."

They begin to make their way back to the swamp.

"R-R-R-A-RRRR!" growls a deep, raspy voice behind them.

"Uh-oh," whispers Mario.

Six real Mega Moles scamper up to the plumbers and surround them. Mario and Luigi stand there motionless, afraid to move.

Then one of the eight-foot-tall furry creatures waves its paw under Luigi's nose. When the plumber looks down, he notices that beast is holding a large chocolate-chip cookie.

"For me?" Luigi asks nervously.

"Rrarrr," replies the monster. Pushing the cookie into Luigi's mouth, he licks his face.

Another Mega Mole lurches forward and presents Mario with a pawful of shiny coins.

"Gee, thanks," says Mario. He drops the coins into a fold in his costume.

Soon, the plumbers and their newfound friends are ambling back to the swamp, arm in arm. They sing some old plumbing songs together and exchange cookie recipies.

"This is great," says Luigi cheerfully. "First we'll go to their cave and load up on emergency supplies. Then we'll get these monsters to help us bust into the castle."

"R-rr-arrr," says a woolly, brown Mega Mole.

***The plumbers collect 10 coins.***

If you think the plumbers should follow the Mega Moles, turn to page 98.

If you think they should turn back to the ship instead, turn to page 25.

# 4

Luigi counts his money carefully and is pleased to find that he has more than enough. Eagerly, he bounces up to the shabby wooden snack stand.

"That'll be five coins, sir," says the wiry, red-and-blue haired turtle at the popcorn stand.

Luigi hands him five coins.

The attendant hands him an empty paper bag.

"Hey!" shouts Luigi, glaring at the weightless package in his hands. "There's nothing in this thing!"

"Hmmm," says the turtle. "I could check to see if that's really true, but it'll cost you another five coins."

"What?" Luigi screams. "Five! That's highway robbery!"

After standing there, scowling at the attendant for three whole minutes, however, his stomach starts to rumble.

"Okay, okay!" Luigi says, handing the attendant five more coins and the empty bag.

"You're right," says the skinny turtle. He studies the paper bag thoughtfully. "I guess you must have bought a bag of air by mistake."

"Huh?" says Luigi. "I didn't—"

"Tell you what I'll do," the weasel-faced turtle suggests, placing one greasy paw on the plumber's shoulder. "Give me five more coins, and I'll fill your bag with popcorn, absolutely free!"

"Well, gee." Luigi scratches his head. "I guess that sounds like a good deal."

Trudging back to his seat in the big tent, Luigi notices that the popcorn is extremely stale. He shoves the uneaten bag into his pocket and wonders if he should have bought some pretzels instead.

***The plumbers now have a bag of popcorn but they lose 15 coins.***

Turn to page 118.

# 5

"**N**o problem, Your Highness," says Mario cheerfully. "If there's one thing that I can do well, it's—"

"Brag?" Luigi interrupts.

"Never mind," Mario grumbles. After glaring at his brother for a few moments, he begins to scale the tall, narrow tree. In no time at all, he's standing on the very top branch. He plucks the tickets from the mouth of a surprised Cheep Cheep, waves them triumphantly, then tucks them into his pocket.

"Aaawrk!" The Cheep Cheep squawks furiously and dives at Mario's head.

The nimble plumber bounds into the air and lands feet-first on the vicious creature's back. Poof! It vanishes with one last screech. But Mario isn't out of trouble yet.

"He's coming down the fast way," observes the king as the plumber plummets groundward. Luigi covers his eyes.

Mario grabs hold of a protruding branch as he shoots past, executes a neat gymnastic twirl, and then hauls himself to a standing position. The king applauds enthusiastically.

"Nice going, big brother," Luigi calls.

"I know," Mario agrees.

From his vantage point high in the air Mario can see the giant tent of the Dino-Flying Derby. But he can also see a mysterious fortress in a nearby swamp, and something large and green moving along the edge of the desert.

"Hmmm," he says thoughtfully. "Lots of things seem worth investigating. But I'd really hate to miss the Derby."

### Solve this puzzle for some advice:

• If Mario had binoculars with him, this is what he would see:

To help decide where the plumbers should go next, find the scene that would fit perfectly with Mario's view.

***The plumbers now have the tickets.***

If you think they should go to the Derby right away, turn to page 113.

If you think they should explore the edge of the desert, turn to page 12.

If you think they should head to the swamp, turn to page 65.

**6**

"We'll head toward the desert," shouts Mario from his high perch. "I want to know what that big green thing is. Besides, I see some tracks heading that way." With his plunger, he gestures toward a narrow trail of reptilian footprints that wind westward into the island's bleak desert.

Mario quickly climbs down from the tree. Side by side, he and Luigi examine the line of three- and four-toed tracks.

"Yep," the tall, skinny plumber muses, scratching his chin thoughtfully. "These prints definitely came from a—hey!"

He catches a glimpse of Toad stumbling aimlessly toward the patch of ferocious Muncher plants. Just in time, the plumber dashes over and grabs the royal mushroom retainer by the collar of his red velvet vest.

"What are you doing?" Luigi asks, holding Toad a few inches above the ground.

"Cookies," Toad says brightly. He reaches toward the flat, circular heads of the Munchers. The deadly plants stand motionless. Their wide eyes watch him eagerly.

"Your Majesty," Mario says with concern, "I think one of us had better take Toad back to the ship, before he gets himself in real trouble."

"I don't know," muses the mushroom monarch, who is reclining on a nearby stone. "That sounds like work." He takes out a silver comb and begins to fuss with his beard.

"Don't worry, Your Highness," says Mario. "I'll take him home. But while I'm gone, I'll need you to protect Luigi from all the creatures that may lurking about."

"I resent—" an indignant Luigi starts to say. But Mario shushes him with a secret plumbers' hand-sign.

Mario squints and shields his eyes with one hand. He points toward the desert dramatically. "Look over there!" he shouts. "I think I see some Mega Moles coming this way!"

"I'm sorry, Mario. I'd love to protect Luigi, but I don't have time," says the king quickly, putting his comb back into a flap in his robe. "I must accompany Toad back to the ship right away." The monarch walks briskly up to the mushroom retainer. "After all, uh, I'm the only one who's counted all the steps up the gangplank. Without me, Toad could—well, stub one of his toes or something...goodbye."

Without wasting another second, the king grabs one of Toad's hands and begins to lead the bewildered mushroom off to the S.S. Moreltania. They soon disappear into the distance.

Alone now, the two plumbers head for the desert.

**Turn to page 51.**

"**Aha!**" shouts Mario cheerfully. "I knew there was a reason we brought this along."

From his pocket, he takes out the silver flashlight that he grabbed when he first left the ship. Bravely, he and Luigi begin to make their way down the steep stone steps.

Most people never think of checking the batteries in flashlights. So there's usually no way to know how long their power will last when you need them.

Neither plumber checked these batteries, either.

After ten steps, the flashlight dies. Mario and Luigi are plunged into darkness.

Unfortunately, the Mega Moles that live at the bottom of the stairs can see perfectly well in the dark.

Lights out.

**GAME OVER!**

15

# 8

"Bwarooo! Bwarooo!" Luigi howls as they trudge out of the ship. "Look at me, I'm a big Brachiosaurus."

"Hush," says Mario from the rear of the costume. "And watch where we're going."

"Hee-hee! This is fun!" Luigi continues. "Bwarooo! Bwarooo! Bwa—"

"What's going on?" Mario asks after the sudden silence.

"Uh, big brother," Luigi mumbles. "There's another dinosaur in front of us, and I think it's a real one."

If Mario could look through the front of the costume right now, he'd see a huge, hungry Tyrannosaurus Rex.

**Solve this puzzle to find out what happens next:**

• Yikes! This hungry beast will eat just about anything. Look at his teeth carefully. Can you guess which of these trees has been bitten by the ferocious monster? Be careful! If you choose incorrectly, the Super Mario Bros. will be up against something they didn't bargain for.

**If you think tree A was bitten by the Tyrannosaurus, turn to page 88.**

**If you think tree B was bitten by the Tyrannosaurus, turn to page 41.**

# 9

Mario looks at his brother. "Well, he did say smash them," he says with a smile.

"One, two, three, go!" shouts Luigi.

At the same time, each plumber reaches into his pocket and takes out a plunger. They each swing them at a skeleton.

With a splintering crash, both monsters shatter into hundreds of pieces.

"Well done," says Mario.

He and Luigi wink at each other. Then they bow, shake hands, and perform the Secret Plumbers' Handshake.

Unfortunately, while all that is happening, the evil bones have rearranged themselves into one big skeleton.

CRASH! BASH!

The horrid creature knocks the plumbers unconscious with its bony fists.

An hour or so later, they wake to find themselves somewhere back in the giant maze.

"Oh no!" screams Luigi. "No! No! No! No! No!"

"What's wrong?" Mario asks, nervously.

"Never mind," Luigi answers. "For a moment I thought I lost my bag of cookies." He reaches into his overalls to make sure that they are still there. "I only dropped a bunch of coins."

***The plumbers lose 15 coins.***
Turn to page 110.

# 10

Luigi stops in his tracks. He grabs his brother by the arm.

"Popcorn!" he shouts.

"Awww, come on," moans Mario. "We're lost in a maze and all you can think of is eating?" Annoyed, he begins to trudge down the lane, away from his younger brother.

"No," says Luigi cheerfully. "We can use the popcorn to mark a trail. Then we'll know if we've travelled on any of these paths already."

"Great idea," says Mario, taking out the paper bag containing the popcorn. "If I didn't know you better, I'd swear you were a genius." He slaps Luigi on the back.

"Gee, thanks a lot," Luigi says sarcastically.

Scattering popcorn as they go, the plumbers soon make great progress into the heart of the giant labyrinth.

"Just one thing," Luigi adds. "If we run out of popcorn, don't even think of using my cookies."

A few minutes later, Mario and Luigi have made their way to the very center of the maze.

**Turn to page 31.**

21

# 11

"This way," Luigi says confidently. The two plumbers follow the trail of dinosaur tracks that leads down the slippery, marshy hillside.

"Watch your step, little brother," Mario calls to Luigi, who is several yards ahead of him. "The ground looks very slip—"

He falls forward onto the ground.

Luigi bounces back toward him and helps him up.

"What did you say?" he asks.

"Never mind," grumbles Mario. "I think I see something up ahead."

At the bottom of the hill, a weird collection of granite statues is spread out through the steamy, swampy area. Most are images of strange monsters that Mario and Luigi have never seen before, but one or two look oddly familiar.

"Wait a minute!" shouts Luigi as he examines one of the strange granite blocks. "This is no unidentifiable statue. It's Yoshi!"

Sure enough, the six-foot-tall dinosaur has been petrified. He's been frozen into a solid block of stone, with a terrified expression on his face.

"It looks like he was running from something," says Mario.

"Don't worry, pal," says Luigi, patting the stone dinosaur on the muzzle. "We'll get you back to normal."

Then he spots a bag of cookies at Yoshi's feet.

"I don't suppose you'll be needing these for a while," Luigi says, and pockets the chocolate-chip treats.

"Over here!" shouts Mario.

A few feet beyond Yoshi is a stone statue of a pretty young girl with curly hair dressed in a formal ball gown. Her tiara is tilted back and her right leg is stretched forward as if she, too, were running from something.

"Princess Toadstool!" gasps Luigi.

Then, over the princess's shoulder, he spots an eerie yellow light. About a quarter of a mile away, the windows of a dark fortress glow through steamy wisps of swamp gas.

His brother sees it too. "Come on, Luigi," says Mario grimly.

Silently, the plumbers begin to march towards the hulking, dark building.

**Turn to page 50.**

24

# 12

The Super Mario Bros. can be silly sometimes, but they're not stupid.

The moment the horrible, fuzzy monsters get a few feet ahead of them, Mario and Luigi scramble away.

"Wow!" pants Mario, as they dash back to the ship. "These costumes worked a little too well."

They march back to the S.S. Moreltania and grab the Brachiosaurus costume instead.

**Turn to page 67.**

# 13

Louder than thunder on a stormy night, the giant, charging Dino Rhinos blast into the four heroes and crash through them.

Miraculously, no one is hurt.

"That was quite rough," says the king, straightening his crown.

"Hey! Our tickets!" shouts Mario.

Somehow, Mario and Luigi's tickets have been speared by one of the stampeding monster's horns.

Already a good thirty yards away, the pack of rambling beasts swerves from the road and heads out into the sandy orange desert.

"After them!" shouts Luigi.

"Is that really necessary?" asks the king. "I'm feeling a bit fatigued."

**Solve this puzzle for some advice:**

• Do you think it's possible to trace a path all the way to the end without stepping on the same number twice? You may not move diagonally. If you think it can be done, send the plumbers after the Dino Rhinos. If you think it's not possible, don't let them go.

| 1 | 16 | 7 |
| 15 | 2 | 3 |
| 1 | 3 | 8 |
| 6 | 9 | 5 |
| 4 | 12 | 13 |
| 6 | 8 | 8 |
| 9 | 3 | 5 |
| 10 | 17 | 2 |
| 8 | 7 | 15 |
| 11 | 14 | 1 |
| 15 | 3 | 7 |

▲ START ▲

***The plumbers no longer have the tickets.***

If you think they should go after the
Dino Rhinos, turn to page 105.

If you think they should just head to the Derby,
turn to page 113.

27

# 14

Magikoopa struggles to grab Luigi, but he simply can't reach far enough under the TV set.

"Let's see," he snarls, standing back up. "Where did I put that old vacuum cleaner?" He walks to the other side of the library and begins to rummage through some old boxes.

"Now's my chance," whispers Luigi. He bolts from underneath the TV and grabs the velvet hem of the evil magician's hat.

ZAP! SPAK! SIZZLE!

Three quick jolts of electricity shock the tiny plumber.

"Ouch!" he wails. Now he's the size of a raisin.

ZAP!

Another bolt of energy shoots out from the pointy top of the horrible hat and whooshes in a tight circle around Luigi. It doesn't touch him, though. Instead it heads straight for the unconscious Mario.

Terrified, Luigi watches as his brother

shrinks down to the size of Magikoopa's smallest toenail.

Then everything goes black.

**Turn to page 92.**

# 15

The plumbers continue to wind aimlessly through the maze of hedges, boards and stone walls. But after fifteen more minutes, they still haven't made any progress.

Then Luigi stops walking and grabs his brother by the arm. "I've got a plan," he says, taking a fistful of coins out of his pocket.

Slowly he leads Mario through the maze, leaving a coin on the ground every few feet.

After about five minutes, Luigi stops again and stares at his brother for a moment.

"What are you doing?" asks Mario.

"Gee, I forget," Luigi answers. "But I bet it was a really great idea."

With a few less coins in their pockets, the plumbers continue through the maze.

***The plumbers lose 7 coins.***
Turn to page 90.

# 16

"This is it?" asks Mario, as he and his brother look around them.

In heart of the maze is a small yard, about twenty feet across. And in the center of that clearing stands a small stone hut, about eight feet wide.

Cautiously, the two plumbers tiptoe into the small, dark shack. Inside they find nothing but one, long, torch-lit staircase. Without pausing, they head down into the dim, mysterious depths.

"I feel funny," says Luigi, walking a few feet behind his brother.

"Ugh," says Mario. "Do you really have to tell jokes right now? I'm not—"

When he turns to look at his brother, though, he stops in his tracks. Luigi's hair is standing straight up. His mustache is fanned out like a bushy black porcupine.

"Must be a lot of static electricity in the air, or something," says Luigi. The tall, skinny plumber struggles to stuff all of his hair back under his green cap. After a few seconds, however, he gives up. They continue on their way.

They descend deeper and deeper into the earth. Finally, the staircase ends and the Mario Bros. head down an enormous stone hallway.

"Where exactly are we headed?" asks Luigi after about fifteen minutes of marching and marching past torches and nothing else.

"We're going to find out who turned the princess and Yoshi into stone," Mario says with determination. He straightens his red plumber's cap and adjusts the straps on his overalls. "And then we're going to get our money back from that crummy festival," he adds.

Just then, a block of stone drops from the ceiling. Mario dives backwards just in time to avoid being squashed into a big, flat plumber pancake. Jumping to his feet, he peers down at the stone block. It leers back up at him out of tiny, knowing eyes.

"Thwomp trap!" Mario gasps.

Luigi studies the course ahead of them. In order to continue, the plumbers will have to dodge several medium-sized falling stone Thwomp traps and a giant Thwomp smasher.

"Good," he says. "I was beginning to get a little bit bored."

**Solve this puzzle to find out what happens next:**

• One of these ropes will lower a bridge so the
plumbers can get through the obstacle course.
The other will drop a ten-ton Thwomp on top of
them. Which rope should they pull?

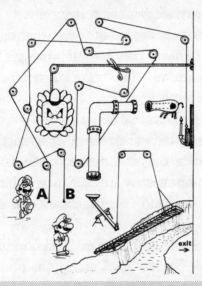

**If you think they should pull rope A,
turn to page 112.**

**If you think they should pull rope B,
turn to page 48.**

# 17

Mario and Luigi do some quick plumber-ome-try on their fingers. Then they exchange glances.

"Too heavy!" they exclaim together.

The plumbers don't wait to see what the evil skeletons do next. They take off running.

"Where are we going?" asks Luigi, a few feet behind his brother.

"Trust me," says Mario.

He races to the wall on the other side of the library, with the bony monsters only a few feet behind him. Just as they are about to grab him, he opens a door marked "broom closet" and ducks down.

The skeletons go flying over Mario's head and land inside the closet. Quickly, the plumber shuts the door and locks it.

"Grrr," snarls Magikoopa. "Everyone always uses that trick."

Then, before the plumbers can catch their breath, he waves his wand again.

"Six, eight, ten, blast again!"

Two more blue fireballs zoom across the room. One hits Mario in the chest. He falls to the ground, unconscious.

Luigi barely manages to dive out of the way. He lands sideways on the library's tile floor with a loud crunch.

"My cookies!" the plumber screams. "You made me crush my cookies!" His eyes narrow to two furious slits. "Now it's personal," he says in a menacing whisper.

Luigi charges up to the evil turtle. He punches him on the beak so hard that the magician's hat goes flying across the room.

Magikoopa steps backward and stands there, stunned for a moment. Then he lifts his left foot out of its leathery boot and wiggles his big toe at the plumber.

"Seaweed, pumpkin seed, telescope, snow!" he crows.

Instantly, the entire library flashes with blue light.

**Turn to page 58.**

# 18

"No way!" shouts Mario. Before the magician can finish his chant, the plumbers dive to one side. Then they race toward the exit on the other side of the library.

"Kangaroo, bear, over there!" shrieks Magikoopa. In a flash, the giant turtle vanishes. Instantly he reappears in front of Mario and Luigi, blocking their path.

"Now where was I?" he chortles. "Oh yes: Tube sock, alarm clock, oatmeal, sneeze . . . hit the plumbers with a deep, deep freeze!"

A giant snowball appears on the end of Magic Koopa's wand. It hovers there for a moment. Then it flies towards the plumbers.

**If Mario and Luigi have the Fire Flower, turn to page 77.**

**If they do not have the Fire Flower, turn to page 92.**

# 19

Mario, Luigi, the king and Toad begin to wind through the swampy terrain of Dinosaur Island. They follow makeshift, handwritten signs that say "THIS WAY TO DINO-FLYING DERBY," zig-zagging past bubbling tar pits and steaming lava flows.

"Stay on the path, everyone!" Mario advises. He takes his emergency plunger out of his back pocket and uses it to beat back a couple of evil Pokey cactus plants that are attempting to slide onto the trail.

As they continue onward, past herds of barking Triceratopses and flocks of other dinosaurs, a strange rumbling sound begins to fill the air.

"What's that?" asks the King.

"I think it's my stomach," says Luigi. "Yoshi got most of the cookies and I'm—"

"Be quiet, little brother," Mario advises.

All four heroes turn and look behind them. Luigi's stomach isn't what's causing the rumbling. Instead, a herd of giant rhinoceros-like dinosaurs is charging up the path towards them.

"Dino Rhinos!" shout the plumbers.

"Everyone, jump to the side!" commands Mario.

"Or get squishified!" Luigi adds.

**Solve this puzzle to find out what happens next:**

• This herd of Dino Rhinos is about to charge and flatten everything in its path. Can you decide which bush is safe from the stampeding monsters?

Study the back of each beast. The number next to each arrow will tell you how many spaces it will move in each direction before switching to the next arrow.

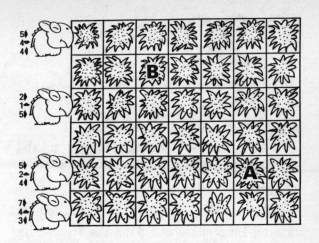

**If you think bush A is safe, turn to page 46.**

**If you think bush B is safe, turn to page 26.**

# 20

"Watch this," says Luigi, scurrying up the tree. "Just like taking candy from a—"

Snap!

A Cheep Cheep swoops down from the nest and bites Luigi on the end of his nose.

"Yowtch!" the plumber screams and lets go of his branch. He tumbles down into a Muncher patch below the nest.

Snap! Snap! Snap!

Hundreds of hungry plants bite and snap and snag Luigi. It takes him a full fifteen minutes to crawl out of the grisly garden.

"Hmmm," says the king. "Maybe you should try that, too, Mario."

"Nah," the plumber replies. He casts a glance at his battered brother. "I think, right now, it's best if we all go back to the ship and gather several hundred bandages."

**GAME OVER!**

# 21

"Surprise!" shout two voices from inside the Tyrannosaurus.

It wasn't a real dinosaur, either.

Instantly, two gigantic armored turtles burst through the fabric of the costume.

"It's the Hammer Brothers," squeals Luigi as the horrible monsters race up to him.

Mario and Luigi fumble frantically for the zipper inside their costume, but it is too late.

With his green, blubbery right arm, one enormous turtle picks up the two plumbers—still inside their Brachiosaurus costume—and holds them high in the air.

The other turtle takes out a large bottle of rubber cement and glues the costume's zipper shut.

"This is a treat," remarks the elder Hammer Brother as he lumbers home with the helpless plumbers slung over his shoulder.

The other giant turtle follows a few feet behind him. "And it's so convenient when lunch-meat comes in these easy-to-store packages," he laughs.

**GAME OVER!**

**22**

Without straying, the two super plumbers stump directly back to the cruise ship.

"We're back, Your Majesty," announces Mario, as he and Luigi race onto the deck of the S.S. Moreltania. "How's Toad doing?"

"Toad?" the mushroom monarch asks.

"Yes. I hope he's feeling better," Mario says hurriedly. "Anyway, we need some costumes so we can sneak into a fortress in the swamp."

"Swamp?" asks the king.

"Yeah," says Luigi. "We think we'll be able to disguise ourselves and make our way under the fortress walls."

"Walls?" asks the king, dully.

"Oh no!" Mario wails. "Not you, too! Toad's amnesia must be contagious."

Mario grabs his brother and leads him quickly away from the king, before Luigi too starts to forget everything. Luigi has always been very susceptible to bouts of amnesia.

He leads Luigi down a flight of stairs and into a large open storage room. A sign above the door says "COSTUMES. Warning: Many of these do not float."

"No way!" gripes Luigi, spying a tutu and some giant clown shoes. "I'm not dressing up like a ballerina again, ever!"

"Relax," says Mario. He holds up two large costumes. One is covered with matted grey fur. The other is green and shiny.

"So what are we going to be?" he asks. "Giant moles? Or a great big Brachiosaurus?"

## Solve this puzzle for some advice:

• Unscramble the letters beneath each costume or disguise and write them in the spaces below each one. The circled letters will spell out the costume that the plumbers should wear.

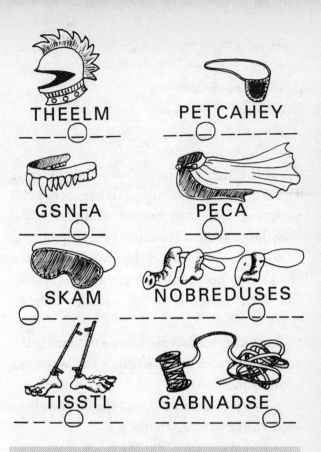

THEELM

PETCAHEY

‐ ‐ ‐ ‐ ‐ ‐ ‐ 〇 ‐

‐ ‐ 〇 ‐ ‐ ‐ ‐ ‐

GSNFA

PECA

‐ ‐ ‐ ‐ ‐ 〇 ‐

‐ ‐ ‐ 〇 ‐

SKAM

NOBREDUSES

〇 ‐ ‐ ‐ ‐

‐ ‐ ‐ ‐ ‐ ‐ 〇 ‐ ‐

TISSTL

GABNADSE

‐ ‐ ‐ ‐ ‐ 〇

‐ ‐ ‐ ‐ ‐ ‐ 〇 ‐

**If you think the plumbers should disguise them-
selves as giant moles, turn to page 5.**

**If you think they should disguise themselves as
a dinosaur, turn to page 67.**

# 23

R-R-R-UMBLE! The pack of six stampeding Dino Rhinos charges straight up the narrow dirt path. Just in time, all four heroes dive out of the way. Luigi and Toad land in a patch of pale blue swamp moss to the left of the trail. Mario grabs the king by his purple velvet collar and yanks him to the right, just missing a hungry Piranha plant sapling.

The bulky monsters blast past, leaving behind a trail of dust, loose dirt clods and some small round objects.

"Cookies?" Toad asks, pointing to the shiny coins scattered about the path.

"No," says Luigi. "But these are great, too." Quickly, he and his brother gather all of the coins.

"It's a good thing those Rhinos charged just then," says Mario, pocketing his share of the money. "So we won't have to charge anything later."

Climbing back onto the trail, they continue on their way, following the signs for the festival.

***The plumbers collect 15 coins.***
Turn to page 113.

Turn to page 113.

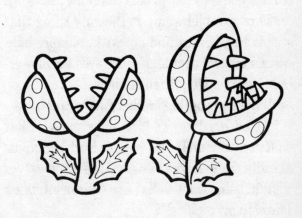

# 24

With a hop, a skip, and a jump, Mario crosses the lowered bridge and dives under the first stone booby trap.

Wham! The Thwomp crashes to the ground, too late. "Mmrrrr," it growls furiously.

While it's down, Luigi vaults over it.

"That's one," laughs Mario.

The next two prove just as easy. The plumbers make it past without a scratch. But the last one is too big to beat that way.

"This giant Thwomp is the only thing that stands between us and . . . well . . . more hall-ways, I guess," says Mario. He eyes the glowering stone monster. Then he sighs.

"What's wrong, big brother?" asks Luigi.

"We need a decoy." Mario sighs again. "Shut your eyes, Luigi. This is going to hurt," he advises sadly. Then he reaches for Luigi's cookies.

"What—no way!" yells Luigi. "No one's gonna Thwomp my cookies!"

Mario grabs for the bag. Luigi jumps back. His fingers catch in Mario's pocket.

R-r-r-i-i-p-p!

"Aaugh!" screams Mario, as a shower of golden coins flies out of his torn pocket. Several roll under the Thwomp trap.

THWOMP!

"My coins," moans Mario.

"Go!" shrieks Luigi. He shoves Mario over the trap while it's still down.

"My coins," wails a stricken Mario. "My—" He stops short, and his eyes open wide with joy. "Coins!"

There at the plumbers' feet are hundreds of coins. Most have been stomped completely flat by the Thwomp over many years and are of no use to anyone. But Mario sifts through the flattened disks and picks out a few that have survived the pounding.

Then he and Luigi press on down the torchlit, static electricity-charged hall.

***The plumbers lose 20 coins, but collect 30 more. They gain 10 coins.***

Turn to page 89.

# 25

The plumbers wade through ponds and puddles, dodging Muncher plants and brushing away swarms of marsh bugs. Eventually they reach the mysterious fortress.

"There's no way in," sighs Luigi, studying the fort's high stone walls.

"I doubt that," says Mario. "Finding a way in is usually not a big problem. Let's just hope there's a way to get out."

Carefully, the plumbers walk around the entire fortress, studying the smooth rock walls. But there don't seem to be any gaps.

"Hmmm," Mario ponders. "These walls look too steep to climb. But there's just got to be some way to get to the other side."

**If the plumbers have the Magic Feather, turn to page 115.**

**If they do not have the Magic Feather, turn to page 103.**

# 26

"We should definitely go this way," Mario says, pointing. He and Luigi follow the dinosaur tracks into the desert. As they continue, however, the whole scene begins to take on a sense of familiarity. It also begins to take on a truly unpleasant odor.

"Ugh," says Mario, wrinkling his nose at the smell of moldy cheese and rotting orange peels. "We must be getting near the Valley of the Koopas."

Sure enough, a wooden, arrow-shaped sign says: KOOPA VALLEY DEAD AHEAD. DEAD ABODY, TOO, IF YOU'RE NOT CAREFUL.

Sitting on a rusty, dented trash can nearby is Bowser Koopa, king of the wicked monster turtles that infest the Mushroom Kingdom and, lately, Dinosaur Island. He is busy using a rusty metal file to scuff up his fingernails.

Mario and Luigi trudge up to him through the dirty yellow sand.

"What do you plumbers want?" he snarls.

"We're looking for Yoshi and Princess Toadstool," says Luigi.

"Never heard of 'em," snaps Bowser. "Now go away, I'm busy."

The two plumbers look at him suspiciously for a moment. Then they wave their pinkies at each other three times. That's the secret plumber hand-signal for "I think the giant turtle is lying."

"What's in the can?" asks Mario.

"Nothing for you," growls the evil turtle king. "And you have just ten seconds to get out of here, or you're both in big trouble. Ten, nine, eight, five, four, three, one! Too late!"

Before Mario and Luigi have a chance to correct Bowser's math, the giant turtle lifts the lid off of the rusty trash can and dumps out four hideous, whirring robot monsters. They look a little bit like dinosaurs, and also a little bit like lawn mowers.

"These are three of my Mecha-Koopas," laughs Bowser.

Once again, the plumbers have no time to correct the evil turtle's counting. Steadily, the monsters grind toward them, whirling and flailing their razor-sharp claws.

## Solve this puzzle to find out what happens next:

• Bowser Koopa has built an army of Mecha-Koopas. If Mario and Luigi can figure out how the robots are put together, they'll have a better idea of how to fight them. Can you tell which parts Bowser used? Here is a complete Mecha-Koopa:

**A**  **B**

If you think he used group A, turn to page 100.
If you think he used group B, turn to page 83.

# 27

FWOOSH! FWOOSH!

Two more fireballs sail after Mario and Luigi, one after the other.

Not even close.

"Take us down!" shouts Luigi.

"Right you are," answers Mario.

Before the creepy magician can do anything else to bother the plumbers, they have landed softly on the ground inside the fortress.

"I'm glad that guy's gone," says Luigi, looking back up at the towering stone walls.

"I'm not so sure," Mario replies. "Creeps like that usually tend to show up later on in an adventure."

Side by side, the plumbers march into the courtyard.

**Turn to page 80.**

# 28

Mario takes the pair of tickets out of his overalls pocket and hands them to the grumpy green
guard.

"Oh," the guard mutters, sounding even more
irritated. He drops the two passes into his buck-
et. "You did have tickets after all. They must be
letting everyone into these things nowadays."
He steps to one side.

"Gee, what a grouch," says Luigi as they enter.

Inside, the two plumbers are sadly disappointed.

There are nowhere near three-dozen exciting
attractions, as the advertisements had
promised. Instead, a handful of rickety rides are
scattered about the area. Many of them aren't
even running and almost all of the light bulbs
seem to be burned out.

Off to one side a crummy little ferris wheel
stands still. Apparently, no one even bothered
to plug it in. There are no cotton candy ma-

chines. There is no orchestra. There is only a small popcorn cart and one big circus tent in the center of the field. And only two or three dozen people have showed up to see the Derby at all.

"Boy," says Mario, as he and Luigi wander into the big tent. "What a cheesy festival."

"Don't say that word," snaps Luigi. "I'm hungry."

Inside, the International Dino-Flying Derby turns out to be even crummier. Again, most of the light bulbs in the area are flickering weakly. And in the stands, most of the audience seems to be made up of Koopa Troopas, Mega Moles and other dangerous characters.

"Are you sure this place is safe?" asks Mario, sitting down next to the king.

"I hope nobody tries to steal my jewel-encrusted sandals," says the mushroom monarch.

But none of the monsters seem to notice him. Instead, all eyes are upon a skinny reptile in a tattered top hat now standing in the center of the tent.

"Ladies and gentlemen," wheezes the creature. "Here we go!"

Slowly, a few sickly dinosaurs begin to make their way onto center stage. One by one, they flap their wings and lift themselves off of the ground for a few seconds. A couple of the monsters in the audience clap their hands once or twice.

"Gee," says Luigi. "This is really thrilling." He stands up from his uncomfortable wooden bench. "Can I go get some popcorn?"

"I'm not sure we have enough money," Mario answers. "But if you do go, be sure to come right back. Yoshi and the princess were supposed to be competing, and I don't see them anywhere. We might have to do some instant investigation."

**If the plumbers have 15 or more coins, turn to page 7.**

**If they have fewer than 15 coins, turn to page 118.**

# 29

Suddenly, Magikoopa is towering high above Luigi's head.

"You got bigger!" gasps the plumber, stepping backward.

"Guess again!" laughs the evil magician.

Luigi stumbles over a crack between the floor tiles. The gap is up to his waist!

"I've been shrunk!" he wails.

The turtle reaches down with his huge, slimy paw and tries to grab the plumber, but Luigi dives out of the way.

Magikoopa picks up his empty shoe and begins to pound it on the floor to squash him. But Luigi is too quick. He dodges the giant, slamming shoe and runs into the space underneath the magican's television set.

"Come out of there," grunts the turtle. He crouches down and tries to reach Luigi, but his hands are too big to fit under the TV. "Come out of there right now!"

"No way," shouts Luigi.

Behind Magikoopa, he can see that Mario is still out cold. He also notices that the sorcerer's magic hat is lying on the ground only a few inches from the TV.

"Boy," Luigi mutters. "If I could get at that, then you'd see some fireworks."

Unfortunately, when you're the size of a prune, a few inches can seem like miles.

**Solve the puzzle on the next page for advice.**

• Look carefully at Magikoopa's hat. There's a secret message on it! Just follow the three guidelines below, and you'll get a clue about what Luigi should do next.

1) Change the letters inside triangles to O's.
2) Cross out all the letters inside stars.
3) Read everything backward.

**If you think Luigi should try to grab the hat,
turn to page 28.**

**If you think Luigi should stay put,
turn to page 4.**

# 30

The turtle magician dives into the TV, and begins to chase Luigi around the inside of the set.

"Help! Help!" Luigi screams as the turtle closes in on him. "Mario! Wake up!"

Across the room, on the library floor, Mario opens his eyes. He spies the bizarre scene inside the television. Magikoopa has grabbed Luigi by the throat.

Wasting no time, Mario reaches into his overalls pocket and takes out the remote control. He presses the first button he sees.

WHOOSH!

A giant bowling ball sails over Luigi and Magikoopa's heads.

"Huh?" gasps the turtle, looking up.

A deep voices blares from the TV speaker: "It's time for BOWLING FOR BILLIONS!"

With all his might, Luigi leaps high into the air. He grabs the top of the TV set and pulls himself out of the opening there.

CRASH!

A ball slams into Magikoopa. He tumbles to the bottom of the TV like a bowling pin.

"Strike!" the announcer's voices bellows. "You win the money!"

Instantly, hundreds of shiny coins begin to fountain out of the top of the TV set.

"Ya-hoo!" shouts Luigi. He jumps down to the library floor and begins to gather the money. "We're rich!"

"Help! Ack! No more!" moans Magikoopa, as a pile of heavy bowling pins cascade down onto him.

"Tsk, tsk," says Mario. He aims the remote control at the set once more and pushes the "Off" button.

Balls, pins, and Magikoopa all vanish as the screen goes black.

***The plumbers collect 300 coins.***
Turn to page 74.

# 31

While the two plumbers are still standing in the tent, several reptilian workers take down the big top. Within minutes, everything has been packed up.

"Now what?" asks Mario.

"Maybe we should make tracks," says Luigi.

"Wait a minute," says Mario. "Take a look at these tracks."

Pressed into the muddy ground is a trail of dinosaur footprints. There are far too many of them to have come from the few pathetic creatures in the festival.

"Let's go," Mario commands. He and his brother begin to follow the three-toed prints.

After a few hundred yards, however, the tracks split into two separate branches. One trail leads down a hill and into a steamy swamp. The other winds up on Dinosaur Island's desert.

"Ooooooh!" Luigi begins to sing. "You take the high road and I'll take the low road and I'll—"

"Knock it off!" shouts Mario. "I think we'd better stick together."

"Yeah," says Luigi. "I guess you're right.

"Okay, okay," snaps Mario. "Just help me decide which way we should go next."

**Solve this puzzle to help decide which way Mario and Luigi should go.**

• Here's how the dinosaur footprints begin. Can you figure out which prints will come next?

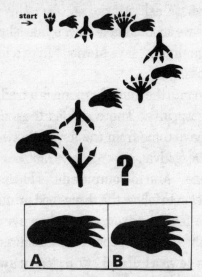

If you think print A comes next, turn to page 22.
If you think print B comes next, turn to page 51.

# 32

Mario, Luigi, Toad and the king begin to trudge down into the steamy, dark swamp.

They don't get very far, however.

"This will not do," says the king. He looks down and notices that the bottom of his purple robe is getting splattered with mud. "I'm going back to the ship. You boys will have to carry on without me."

With that, the monarch turns around, grabs Toad by the hand, and walks back up the hill. The two plumbers are left alone in the swamp.

"How do you like that?" Mario mutters.

"Oh well," says Luigi cheerfully. He holds up his bag of chocolate-chip cookies. "Now we won't have to share these with as many people."

Luigi glances around quickly to make sure that no one around is thinking about trying to make him share his cookies. Then he notices a fresh trail of dinosaur footprints on the ground.

His brother notices them, too.

"This could be interesting," says Mario.

Cautiously, they follow the tracks down the hill and deeper into the swamp.

**Turn to page 22.**

# 33

Mario takes the giant Brachiosaurus costume off its hanger.

"Great," he says cheerfully. "I'll just climb in the front and you can—"

"Oh no you don't!" shouts Luigi. "You be the rear end. I want to be in the front."

"Grow up, will you?" Mario says. "Anyway, this whole plan was my idea. So I get to be in the front."

"Oh, yeah?" whines Luigi. "Well, if I can't be in the front, I'm not going!"

Angrily, the two plumbers stand and scowl at each other for three full minutes without moving, breathing, or even blinking.

### Solve this puzzle to find out what happens next:

• Here are some dinosaur and animal disguises from the costume room. Arrange the hangers by number. Then read the first letter on each tag to get some advice about what the plumbers should do next.

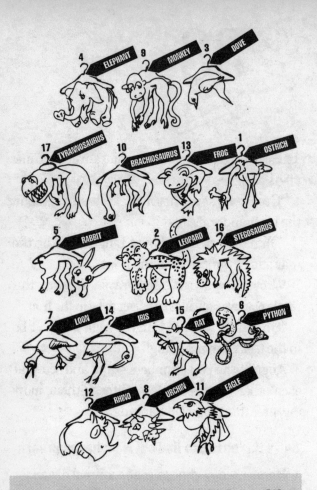

If you think Mario should go in the front of the costume, turn to page 108.

If you think Luigi should be the front half, turn to page 16.

# 34

Magikoopa jumps back down to the library floor.

"This is going to be fun!" he cackles.

He clambers up the front of the TV, reaches up with his now tiny hand and turns a knob.

"Welcome to Wild Whirl Of Sports!" a voice blares from the speaker.

"Eek!" shouts Luigi, as a bobsled filled with mice goes soaring past his head.

SLAM!

A flaming hula hoop flings into his stomach.

CRASH!

Two ultra-heavy football players trample the plumber.

WHOMP!

A miniature elephant wearing a bikini swan-dives on top of Luigi.

"Who needs cable TV?" snickers Magikoopa. "I've got plumbervision!"

**GAME OVER!**

# 35

Mario holds out his empty hands toward the unpleasant green guard.

"We had tickets, sir," he pleads. "But—"

"But what?" snaps the guard.

"We lost them," adds Luigi. "Don't you think you could let us in anyway?" he asks hopefully.

"What kind of a show do you think I'm running here?" roars the guard. "A charity show? A flying-dino free-for-all? A prehistoric public picnic? A no-charge fun show? A cost-free carnival? A not-for-profit . . ."

If the plumbers weren't so busy listening to the guard ramble on about what the dinosaur festival isn't, they'd hear the desperate cries of people being kidnapped and horrible monsters running wild. They would also hear some strange electronic buzzing noises and the sound of people screaming for help.

Unfortunately, the Mario Bros. missed all of that. So there's no way that they can come to

anyone's rescue.  Yoshi, the princess, Toad and
the king are doomed!

**GAME OVER!**

# 36

Mario and Luigi stand very still.

"Maybe if we don't move, he won't see us," Luigi whispers. "I've heard turtles have terrible eyesi—"

ZAP!!

A bolt of rasberry-jam-colored energy blasts the plumbers. At the same moment, Magikoopa shrieks out a word, but the plumbers are too dazed to understand what he's saying. Everything goes red. Then everything goes black.

A few minutes later, Mario and Luigi wake to find that they have been shrunk down to the size of mice! They are both tied to chairs somewhere inside Magikoopa's horrible TV set. Then, strange music starts to play.

"What's the capital of Michigan?" asks a deep mysterious voice.

"Detroit?" Luigi replies.

A loud buzzer sounds.

"Wrong!" the voice blares.

Suddenly, a sack of flour pours onto the plumber's head.

"Oh no!" shouts Mario. "It's a game show!"

For the next seven years, the Mario Bros. are trapped in the TV, answering questions about house plants, old movies, and famous sports stars.

**GAME OVER!**

## 37

The instant the evil magician vanishes, things begin to change.

Zip!

Luigi soars back to normal size.

Zip!

Several pebbles that had been lying around in dusty corners of the library swell rapidly into large granite statues. Then they turn into flesh and blood! A dozen confused dinosaurs stumble out from behind stacks of books and begin to wander out through the doors at the far end of the library.

"I bet Yoshi and Princess Toadstool are snapping out of it, too," says Mario. "Let's get out of this place."

Sure enough, when the plumbers make it back out of the castle, they find Yoshi and the princess waiting for them at the edge of the swamp. "Hooray!" shouts the princess when she spots Mario and Luigi.

"Bwaroo!" Yoshi trumpets joyfully.

Exhausted but happy, all four heroes head back to the ship. "Look!" cries Luigi excitedly.

There on the port bow stand Toad and the king, holding a huge tray of fresh-baked chocolate-chip cookies between them. They seem to have regained their wits ... for now, at least.

"I was really scared," Princess Toadstool confesses as they board the entrance ramp to the big boat. "I thought you boys forgot all about us. We'd have been statues forever!"

"There, there," says Mario, patting her gently on the shoulder. "You know we'd never take you for granite."

**YOU WIN!**
**GAME OVER!**

# 38

$A$t last, the plumbers turn one last corner and emerge at the heart of the maze.

"Yes!" shouts Mario.

"Free at last!" shouts Luigi, waving his monkey wrench triumphantly. "We did it! We made it! We got out! We're free! We're free!"

"Um." Mario tugs at his brother's sleeve. "Don't you think you're overdoing it just a little?"

Ready for anything, now, the two heroes move forward into the fortress's central courtyard.

**Turn to page 31.**

# 39

Just in time, Mario reaches into his pocket and takes out the Fire Flower he picked up on the way out of the ship.

Instantly, he feels his body getting warmer. The moment he's fully charged, he spits.

A fireball shoots out of the plumber's mouth and slams into the giant snowball a few feet away.

With a loud hiss, both balls evaporate into a wisp of steam.

"Spitting is a bad habit, big brother," says Luigi. "But I guess it's okay to do it right now."

"So!" snarls Magikoopa. "You know some tricks of your own!"

"Sure," says Luigi, stepping forward. "Do you have a deck of cards?"

"Silence, fool!" shrieks the giant turtle. Quickly he reaches into his robe and pulls out a handful of old, dry bones. He flings them in front of the plumbers.

"Fork, knife, come to life!" he chants.

The bones begin to swirl around, as if trapped in a miniature tornado. Then they suddenly organize themselves into two huge turtle skeletons.

"Dry Bones. Oh, no!" moans Luigi.

"Smash them!" orders Magic Koopa.

The horrible bone monsters stomp towards Mario and Luigi.

"What do you say, big brother?" whispers Luigi. "Can we handle these boneheads?"

## Solve this puzzle to find out what happens next:

• Mario and Luigi need to know what they're up against. Can you tell which skeleton is heavier? Use the chart at the bottom to find out how much each bone weighs.

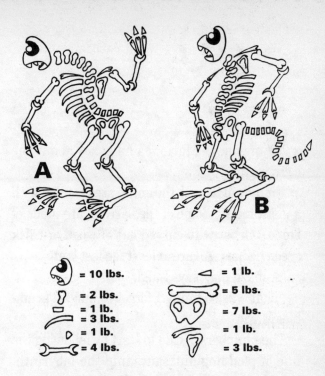

| | | | |
|---|---|---|---|
| = 10 lbs. | | ⊲ = 1 lb. | |
| = 2 lbs. | | = 5 lbs. | |
| = 1 lb. | | = 7 lbs. | |
| = 3 lbs. | | | |
| = 1 lb. | | = 1 lb. | |
| = 4 lbs. | | = 3 lbs. | |

**If you think skeleton A is the heavier one, turn to page 18.**

**If you think skeleton B is heavier, turn to page 34.**

# 40

"Wow," says Mario, as he gazes about the courtyard.

From wall to wall, the entire area is filled with a giant maze. Some of the barriers are made of stone. Others are carved out of wood or thick green hedges. All are at least ten feet high.

"A-maze-ing," says Luigi.

"That was so funny I forgot to laugh," grumbles Mario.

The plumbers decide to start by following the line of plodding dinosaurs into the labyrinth. But in a very short time, that line splits into several confused lines.

Soon, Mario and Luigi are walking by themselves near the middle of the great maze.

"You know," Mario observes. "It never really feels like we've had an adventure until we've wasted a bunch of time wandering around in one of these things."

**If the plumbers have the popcorn,
turn to page 20.**

**If they do not have the popcorn,
turn to page 110.**

# 41

**H**ey! You shouldn't be reading this page! There's no way to wind up here!

Go back to the page that you were just on and try to solve the puzzle—or whatever else you may have been doing—one more time.

# 42

Mario and Luigi are about to run from the clanking metal monsters when Luigi takes a closer look at them. The lead Mecha-Koopa's three legs are all put on at different angles, so it can't move in a straight line. Instead, it advances by walking in wobbly circles.

"Relax," says Luigi, patting his older bother on the shoulder. "Look at these things! They probably can't go more than two miles an—"

ZING! A panel opens on the lead Mecha-Koopa's side and a steel arm reaches out with lightning speed. It slams into the side of Luigi's head. He's out cold.

ZANG! CLANG! Another monster's arm reaches out and hammers Mario into unconsciousness.

"Haw! Haw! Haw!" laughs Bowser. "My monsters sure finished them off quickly."

ZING! One of the Mecha-Koopas bashes the evil turtle king and knocks him out.

Slowly, the squadron of mechanical monsters begins to roll out of the valley. They leave Mario, Luigi and Bowser still lying on the ground. The Mecha-Koopas have much bigger plans.

Today, Dinosaur Island. Tomorrow, the world!

**GAME OVER!**

# 43

Magikoopa lifts his wand and starts to chant. "Soup bone, telephone, alligator, skunk . . ."

"Wait!" shouts Mario. "We only came here to, uh, to borrow some books!"

"You did?" the turtle magican asks. He fiddles with two of the three black hairs on the end of his chin thoughtfully. "Well, I'm using all of them right now!"

"You're reading all the books at once?" asks Luigi.

"Read? Who said anything about reading?" snarls Magikoopa. "I use them as fuel for my electric generator. That's how I can make enough power to run my TV set."

The turtle steps to one side, revealing a giant television console. Affectionately, he rubs one of his giant green paws along the top of the box.

"Someday I'll have cable TV down here. I'll be able to watch hundreds of channels," he continues. "But until then, I have to make my own shows."

Just then, a small, confused dinosaur stumbles in at the other side of the room.

Immediately, Magic Koopa points his wand at the poor creature and shouts:

"Bathtub, sink, dinosaur, shrink!"

A bolt of blue energy leaps from the wand. The dinosaur shrinks down to the size of an apple!

Before, the dinosaur can react, the giant turtle steps forward and grabs him with one hand. Then he lifts up a small flap on top of the TV set and drops him inside.

"Right now, I'm watching a documentary about prehistoric life," he says.

"I see," says Mario, standing on his tiptoes. Inside the TV, the miniscule dinosaur is running around in circles letting out tiny cries of fright.

"You do, eh?" croaks Magic Koopa. "That's too bad. Your nosy friends tried to stop me from using dinosaurs, so I had to turn them into statues. That's what I do to anyone who won't cooperate." He laughs as he straightens his cone-shaped hat. "But I've got bigger, uh, smaller plans for you two."

He whirls around and waves his wand a few inches in front of Mario and Luigi's noses.

"Surfboard, landlord, underwear, dice.

Make these plumbers the size of . . ."

"Uh-oh," says Luigi.

**Solve this puzzle to find out what happens next:**

• There's a secret message hidden in this section of Magikoopa's library. Arrange all the books alphabetically. Then read the last letter in each book's title and you'll find some important advice for the plumbers.

**If you think the plumbers should stay where they are, turn to page 72.**

**If you think the plumbers should try to dive out of the way, turn to page 36.**

# 44

"R-R-R-ROARR!"

The hungry Rex lashes out with one of his razor-sharp claws and tears a hole in the side of the plumbers' costume.

"Run away!" shouts Luigi.

The disguised plumbers break into two halves, and scurry away from the carnivorous beast with all their energy.

The Tyrannosaurus doesn't follow them. Unfortunately, he did rip all the way through to Mario's overalls pocket. As the plumbers run away, they leave a trail of coins scattered on the ground.

Mario is so angry with his brother that he is completely silent as the two of them swap halves of the Brachiosaurus costume.

***The plumbers lose all their coins.***
Turn to page 108.

# 45

Soon the flaming torches that line the walls are gone. Instead, large candles shed a golden light on the stones that lie ahead.

As Mario and Luigi go forward, each set of candles is smaller than the ones before. Eventually, the only candles left are the size of pins. The heroes can barely see two feet in front of themselves.

Suddenly the hallway ends. The only way to go is down. A steep staircase descends into a pitch black opening below.

"Sca-a-a-reee!" says Luigi.

"I'm not afraid of the dark," says Mario, peering into the void. He shivers. "But in this case, I'll make an exception."

**If the plumbers have the flashlight, turn to page 15.**

**If they don't have the flashlight, turn to page 96.**

# 46

The discouraged plumbers round their three-hundreth corner inside the great maze and discover yet another junction. But instead of turning left or right, Luigi walks straight forward. Then he begins to beat his head against the wooden paneled barrier.

"Arrrgh," he wails. "I'm getting confused again!"

Mario pulls his brother away from the wall and shakes him around for a bit.

"Snap out of it," he orders. "We've got princesses and dinosaurs to rescue, so get moving."

Luigi doesn't budge.

"I'll bake you a lasagna when we get back to the boat," Mario adds.

Quickly and silently, the taller, skinnier plumber follows his brother into the next section of the maze.

• Bowser Koopa is about to give this section of the maze a little push. When he does, the plumbers will become more confused than ever! Can you figure out the secret message that will appear when the circle spins around halfway?

If you think the plumbers should go left, turn to page 110.

If you think they should go right, turn to page 76.

# 47

$L$ater on in the week, Magikoopa decides to take a break from working on his TV show. He heads out to one of Dinosaur Island's sandy beaches and relaxes in a hammock near the water's edge.

"Ahhh, this is the life," remarks the evil magician, as he sips a tall glass of onion-ade.

There, in the very center of the ice cube at the bottom of his dirty glass, two raisin-sized objects are frozen solid. Actually, they look a bit like Mario and Luigi.

**GAME OVER!**

# 48

"Land ho!" the king bellows through the ship's intercom. "We'll be arriving at Dinosaur Island in sixty—"

WHAM! The ship lurches to a halt, flinging everyone across the room.

"What happened?" asks Princess Toadstool as her father stumbles down the ship's spiral staircase.

"I have no idea," the Mushroom King answers. "We seem to have run aground. But all the controls said that we were still a mile from the shore."

"Hmmph," Mario grumbles, getting up from the ground. "I could've docked this boat, no problem. Did I ever tell you about the time I managed to float on a giant sponge all the way across Lake Ontario during a—"

"We'd all love to hear your story," the princess interrupts. "But I've got to get Yoshi to the Derby grounds in time to register for the events." She walks across the cabin, pats the round-faced dinosaur on the chin and feeds him a chocolate chip cookie. "He's the two-to-one favorite in the two-legged long jump, you know."

Princess Toadstool and Yoshi head toward the exit plank at the far side of the cabin. "Wish us luck," she cries, waving. "See you after the Derby." Then they head down the plank and are gone.

Soon Mario and the king have shut down all of the ship's engines and are ready to head out to the festival, too.

"Let's go, guys," Mario calls to the others.

"Just a minute," shouts Luigi. Toad still hasn't come to his senses, so the younger plumber has been busy drilling him on the basics.

"This is a wrench," says Luigi, holding up a shiny brass plumbing tool.

"Wrench," Toad repeats dully.

"This is a cookie," says Luigi. He shows the mushroom retainer one of the chocolate chips he managed to retrieve. "If you find any, give them to me."

Finally, the rest of the group gathers at the exit plank and heads down to the banks of Dinosaur Island. Just to be on the safe side, Mario grabs a piece of emergency equipment at the last minute.

"You never know when trouble might surface," he says seriously.

"Good thinking, big brother," says Luigi. "Now let's go to the show!"

**Solve this puzzle for a clue about which piece of equipment the plumbers should take:**

• Examine these bags of cookies. Then choose the bag that should go next.

**A**     **B**     **C**

If you think bag A is correct, do not take the Fire Flower.

If you think bag B is correct, do not take the feather.

If you think bag C is correct, do not take the flashlight.

Turn to page 37.

# 49

"**W**hy didn't we bring a flashlight?" mutters Mario irritably. He leans against one of the stone walls and tries to decide if they should risk walking down the stairs into total darkness. Suddenly, the wall behind him gives way.

"Luigi!" he shouts. "It's a secret passage."

Eagerly, the two plumbers shove the same stone with all their might. The entire wall swings inward with a creak. Wasting no time, they step through the opening.

The air fills with a faint electronic hum as a huge, round room spreads out before the plumbers.

The ceiling is three stories high. Except for a few strange objects in the very center of the room, every table, every corner, every space on every wall is lined with rows and rows of books.

"It's a library," gasps Luigi.

"It's my library," snaps a scratchy, high-pitched voice. A tall, gaunt turtle in a velvet cape slinks toward the plumbers. It's Magikoopa, Bowser Koopa's third cousin twice removed. His long black fingernails reach out menacingly. "And I don't recall inviting either of you," he snarls.

The awful giant turtle adjusts his pointy velvet hat and begins to wave a twisted magic wand at Mario and Luigi.

**Turn to page 85.**

# 50

Four hours later, the plumbers are still relaxing, deep in the Mega Moles' cave.

Luigi's belly is so full of cookies and lasagna, he is almost bursting out of his costume. Still, the Mega Moles continue to shower them with food and gifts.

"Ooooo!" says Mario, examining a shiny purple bowling ball that the monsters have laid at his feet. He rolls it next to his newly acquired TV set and begins to thumb through several of the handsome leather-bound books that the generous creatures have given him.

*"Mega Moles In The Mist,* by Diane Flossy," Mario reads. "'Day Seven: I have made a startling discovery.' Hey, Luigi, listen to this."

The taller, overstuffed plumber looks over at his brother.

"'The giant mole creatures will often befriend others and bring them back to their lair,'" Mario continues to read. "'Once they have been stuffed with a heavy meal of pasta and cakes, the help-less victims will be weighed down and have ab-solutely no way to escape from—' uh-oh!"

**GAME OVER!**

# 51

Whirring and buzzing, the first of the Mecha-Koopas charges up to Luigi. Calmly, the younger plumber takes out his heavy brass monkey wrench and, striking a few strategic blows, smashes the monster into several pieces.

Meanwhile the three other electronic fiends have surrounded Mario. The monsters are too slow to grab him, but he can't escape from them, either.

Then Luigi glances over and notices that Bowser is holding a small object in one hand.

"What's that?" shouts Luigi, racing up to the giant turtle.

"Uh, nothing," says Bowser. He quickly puts his hands behind his back.

"I wouldn't have done that if I were you," says Luigi cheerfully. With one great swing of his wrench, he belts the giant turtle in the stomach.

Bowser howls with pain, drops the strange object on the ground and runs off.

"Come back here, you coward!" shouts Luigi, waving his wrench fiercely. Then he bends over and picks up the strange object.

"It's a remote control," he notes. "Let's see what it can do."

Mario is still busy fending off the other three Mecha-Koopas. But when Luigi points the device at them and presses one of its buttons, the creatures stop dead in their tracks.

"How did you manage that?" asks Mario, panting heavily.

"With this little doo-hickey," says Luigi. "I pushed the OFF button." He twirls his bushy black mustache thoughtfully. "Now let's see what happens if I press button twenty-eight."

"What's twenty-eight?" asks Mario.

"The all-sports channel," Luigi answers. He aims the remote control at the frozen creatures and presses the button.

Sure enough, they spring into action. One mechanical monster reaches out with its iron hand and rips another one's head off. Then the two intact creatures begin to play a clanking, whirring round of volleyball, using the loose head as a ball.

"Personally, I prefer soccer," says Mario, bending over to pick up a few loose coins that the metal monsters have scattered on the ground.

Luigi hands Mario the remote control. Then the two of them turn back out of the desert valley and begin to follow the trail of dinosaur tracks into the swamp.

***The plumbers now have the remote control and they collect 10 coins.***

Turn to page 22.

# 52

The plumbers walk all the way around the fortress again. But they still find no way to get through the massive stone walls.

"I can't stand it!" Luigi starts to whimper. "We're never gonna get in there. We'll never do it. We won't. We can't . . ."

"There, there," comforts Mario, patting his brother gently on the shoulder. "You've got some cookies, remember?"

Immediately, Luigi's expression brightens. He reaches into his pocket and takes a chocolate-chip cookie from the bag. He devours it greedily. Then he begins to calm down.

"We'll find a way in, little brother," says Mario. "You've just got to remember not to panic and—did you say something?"

"What?" says Luigi, licking a few crumbs from his mustache.

"I thought I heard—quick! Over there, behind those rocks!" Mario shouts.

The plumbers race to a cluster of boulders twenty yards out from the castle walls. Climbing them carefully, they peer over the stones into a narrow but deep canyon.

"I knew it!" says Mario.

Twenty feet below, a stream of bewildered dinosaurs is being herded into a tunnel by masked turtle guards.

"What's going on down there?" asks Luigi.

"Beats me," Mario replies. "But I'll bet it has something to do with our petrified friends back by the hill." He scratches his chin thoughtfully. "And I'm sure that tunnel leads inside the fortress."

"So how are we going to get through there?" asks Luigi.

"You just leave that to me," says Mario confidently. He grabs his brother's arm and begins to drag him back up the hill, away from the swamp. "We're going back to the ship to get some disguises," he announces.

**Turn to page 43.**

# 53

"**F**ollow those Rhinos!" Mario shouts. He points his plunger at the stampeding monsters and grabs the king by one of his long purple sleeves. The mushroom monarch is so startled that he forgets to protest.

All four of them race after the mighty herd of charging beasts as they haul out into the desert. Unfortunately, the Dino Rhinos are simply too fast to catch.

Then, far ahead, the gasping heroes see the tickets fly up into the air.

"They're blowing in the wind," Mario observes.

"Yes!" shouts Luigi, watching the passes drift back to them. He beckons with both arms. "Come to papa."

Gently, the tickets float down toward the ground. Mario and Luigi dash forward to grab them.

Bad move!

The racing plumbers stir up a gust of wind that blows the flimsy bits of paper back up toward the sky. They land in a nest, high up in a tree.

An owl-faced Cheep Cheep leans over and snatches the tickets with its beak.

The king looks up at the high nest full of snapping, vicious fish-birds. Then he looks down and studies the wide patch of deadly Muncher plants at the base of the tree.

"It looks easy enough," he says. "Now, which of you two boys is going to go up and get them?"

Mario and Luigi scowl at the king, but neither of them says anything.

**Solve this puzzle to find out what happens next:**

• Look at the two sets of footprints on this tree. The plumber whose shoes match his trail exactly should retrieve the tickets.

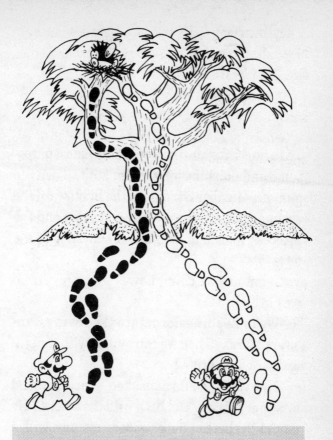

**If you think Mario's shoes match all of the prints in his trail, turn to page 9.**

**If you think Luigi's shoes match his trail, turn to page 40.**

# 54

Mario climbs into the front of the dinosaur costume and pulls the long zipper shut. Then the plumbers lumber back down the hill toward the swamp, past the stone statues of Yoshi and the princess, and on to the strange canyon near the fort.

"What are we doing now?" asks Luigi from way in back.

"We're heading down into the ravine," answers Mario. "Then we can mingle with the other dinosaurs until—"

"Hey you!" shouts a masked, green-skinned dinosaur herder. "Get back with the others." He jabs at the back of the plumbers' costume with a long, pointy spear.

"Ouch!" blurts Luigi.

"Shhhh," whispers Mario. He steers them into the long line of real dinosaurs filing into the tunnel. Soon they are wandering through total darkness.

"What's happening now?" asks Luigi.

"I'm not sure yet," answers Mario.

Just then, they emerge from the tunnel into light.

Quickly, Mario unzips the costume.

"Run for it!" he shouts.

He and Luigi rip from their disguise and dash from the line of dinosaurs. Then they dive around the nearest corner.

After a while, they realize that no one is following them. Carefully, the two heroes step forward to examine their surroundings. They're in a vast stone courtyard.

They've made it inside the fortress at last!

**Turn to page 80.**

109

# 55

The plumbers turn left at the next corner. Then right at the one after that. Then left, then right. Then left, then right. Then left, right, left. Then right, left, right. Then left, right, right, left, left, right, left, right, left—

"Stop!" shouts Mario. "We're lost."

**Solve this puzzle to find out what happens next:**

• Neither of these two maps will help the plumbers get to the center of the maze. But one of them does show the answer to the puzzle on this page. Can you guess which map shows the correct way to reach the center of the triangle?

**If you think Map A is correct, turn to page 90.**

**If you think Map B is correct, turn to page 30.**

# 56

# WHAM!!

## GAME OVER!

# 57

Soon the four heroes reach an open valley with a large, fenced-in area in the middle. Over the top of the wide wooden fence, they can see the upper half of an enormous circus tent. Various squawks, hoots, grunts, and other dinosaur noises drift faintly to their ears.

"This must be the place," says Mario.

"Good," says Luigi. He takes a big sniff of the air. "I smell popcorn."

"Tickets, please," says a large, green guard blocking a space in the wooden wall. A patch on one of his muscular armored arms says "Derby Security."

The king takes two tickets from a pocket in his royal robe and hands them to the guard. Immediately, the big usher shoves him and Toad through the entrance.

"Ouch," says the king. "You don't have to be so pushy." He and Toad disappear inside.

"Well?" asks the guard, glaring at Mario and

Luigi. "Do you two have your tickets, or do I get to get rough?"

**If the plumbers have the tickets,
turn to page 55.**

**If they do not have the tickets, turn to page 70.**

# 58

"**H**ey!" shouts Luigi. "Didn't you bring the Magic Feather along?"

"Good thinking, little brother," says Mario. He reaches into his overalls pocket and takes out the magical item that he grabbed just before leaving the ship.

Instantly, he energizes and a magic cape appears, stuck to his bright red overalls. Filled with super-energy, he grabs his brother by the collar and brings him soaring into the air. Soon, they are higher than the fortress walls and on their way to the other side.

"Hedgehog, bulldog, bicycle tire . . ." a raspy voice murmurs far below them. "Hit them with a red-hot ball of fire!"

"Did you say something, little brother?" asks Mario.

VRROOOM! A blazing fireball soars past the plumbers, nearly setting their shoelaces aflame.

"Yikes!" they both shout.

Far below, leaning out of one of the fortress windows, a giant turtle wearing a pointy magician's cap is peering at them.

"Soap dish, tuna fish, alligator, hen," the creature shrieks. "Blast those plumbers once again!" He ducks his head until the tip of his pointy hat is aimed at the plumbers. With a whoosh, out shoots a fireball, heading straight for Mario and Luigi.

"We're outta here!" shouts Mario. He grabs onto his brother's arm tightly, and zooms into a steep dive.

### Solve this puzzle to find out what happens next:

• If the plumbers know where the danger is, they'll be able to avoid it. You can help them! Study this stream of fireballs carefully. Then try to choose which magical blast is going to come next.

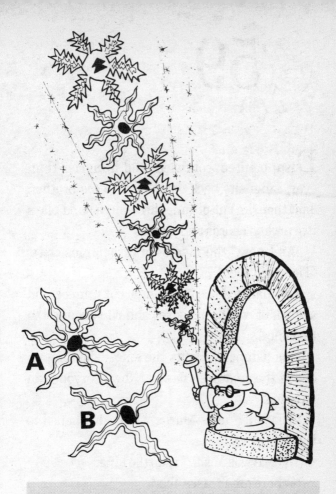

**If you think A is coming next, turn to page 120.**

**If you think B is coming next, turn to page 54.**

# 59

Disappointed, confused, and hungrier than ever, Luigi sits back down next to his brother. Just then, an out-of-tune three-piece band plays two broken chords and stops.

"And now," the master of ceremonies cries. "The main event!"

Five flabby dinosaurs charge out from behind a stack of cardboard boxes and run around the tent once.

"The winner," shouts the emcee, holding up one of the creature's paws. "Now everyone can go home."

"That's it?" asks Mario. "What happened to the flying part?"

"Where was Yoshi?" asks the king.

"Where am I?" asks Toad.

Meanwhile, the rest of the audience has begun to file out of the tent. Mario notices that several large Mega Moles are looking at him and his friends hungrily. Off in one corner, a cluster of Koopa Troopas are waving knives and forks and pointing at Toad.

"Something else is odd, boys," the Mushroom King remarks, not noticing the monsters near-by. "I bought this light-up yo-yo on the way in, and it's acting most peculiar." He dangles the electric toy on the end of its string. Mysteriously, it flickers on and off in a strange pattern.

"I don't know what that means, Your Highness," says Mario. "But you and Toad had better get back to the ship." He cracks his knuckles. "I've got a hunch things are about to get rough around here."

"Yeah," says Luigi. "We'll find your daughter and Yoshi and meet you there soon."

Leading Toad by one hand, the king heads away from the fairgrounds, leaving the two plumbers alone to investigate.

"I've got a funny feeling we're going to have to rescue somebody again," muses Mario.

### Turn to page 63.

# 60

FWOOOSH! The fireball sails toward the plumbers. This time it smacks Mario on the hand—the one holding the Magic Feather.

"Ouch!" Mario wails. The enchanted item vanishes in a puff of blue smoke. So does Mario's cape. The two plumbers drop like a gold-plated blimp.

WHOMP! They slam into the soft, marshy ground, seven stories below.

"Hee, hee!" cackles the magician. He ducks into his window and slams it shut.

"We'll get you later!" Luigi shouts angrily, shaking his fist upward.

Then he and Mario start to search the area around the castle once more. Somewhere, there must be a way to get inside!

***The plumbers lose the Magic Feather.***
Turn to page 103.

# Drip by Drip Scorecard

**Circle each object as you collect it.**

**Keep track of your score here:**

Now, use this chart to find out your P.P.R. Score 10 points for every coin that Mario and Luigi have at the end of this adventure.

Did you meet up with Bowser Koopa? Did you battle the Thwomp? Did you go to the Mega Moles' lair? Try this adventure over again, until you can earn the highest rating.

| | |
|---|---|
| 3600 or more | ← Plumbersaurus Rex |
| King of the Sewer → | 3200 to 3599 |
| | 2000 to 3199 ← Plumber, Second Class |
| Wrench Warmer → | 1000 to 1999 |
| | 999 or less ← Pipesqueak |

121

# A Selected List of Fiction from Mammoth

While every effort is made to keep prices low, it is sometimes necessary to increase prices at short notice. Mandarin Paperbacks reserves the right to show new retail prices on covers which may differ from those previously advertised in the text or elsewhere.

The prices shown below were correct at the time of going to press.

| | | | | |
|---|---|---|---|---|
| ☐ | 7497 0978 2 | **Trial of Anna Cotman** | Vivien Alcock | £2.50 |
| ☐ | 7497 0712 7 | **Under the Enchanter** | Nina Beachcroft | £2.50 |
| ☐ | 7497 0106 4 | **Rescuing Gloria** | Gillian Cross | £2.50 |
| ☐ | 7497 0035 1 | **The Animals of Farthing Wood** | Colin Dann | £3.50 |
| ☐ | 7497 0613 9 | **The Cuckoo Plant** | Adam Ford | £3.50 |
| ☐ | 7497 0443 8 | **Fast From the Gate** | Michael Hardcastle | £1.99 |
| ☐ | 7497 0136 6 | **I Am David** | Anne Holm | £2.99 |
| ☐ | 7497 0295 8 | **First Term** | Mary Hooper | £2.99 |
| ☐ | 7497 0033 5 | **Lives of Christopher Chant** | Diana Wynne Jones | £2.99 |
| ☐ | 7497 0601 5 | **The Revenge of Samuel Stokes** | Penelope Lively | £2.99 |
| ☐ | 7497 0344 X | **The Haunting** | Margaret Mahy | £2.99 |
| ☐ | 7497 0537 X | **Why The Whales Came** | Michael Morpurgo | £2.99 |
| ☐ | 7497 0831 X | **The Snow Spider** | Jenny Nimmo | £2.99 |
| ☐ | 7497 0992 8 | **My Friend Flicka** | Mary O'Hara | £2.99 |
| ☐ | 7497 0525 6 | **The Message** | Judith O'Neill | £2.99 |
| ☐ | 7497 0410 1 | **Space Demons** | Gillian Rubinstein | £2.50 |
| ☐ | 7497 0151 X | **The Flawed Glass** | Ian Strachan | £2.99 |

All these books are available at your bookshop or newsagent, or can be ordered direct from the publisher. Just tick the titles you want and fill in the form below.

**Mandarin Paperbacks**, Cash Sales Department, PO Box 11, Falmouth, Cornwall TR10 9EN.

Please send cheque or postal order, no currency, for purchase price quoted and allow the following for postage and packing:

UK including BFPO £1.00 for the first book, 50p for the second and 30p for each additional book ordered to a maximum charge of £3.00.

Overseas including Eire £2 for the first book, £1.00 for the second and 50p for each additional book thereafter.

NAME (Block letters) ...............................................................................................................

ADDRESS ...............................................................................................................

...............................................................................................................

☐ I enclose my remittance for ........................

☐ I wish to pay by Access/Visa Card Number

Expiry Date